LIFE IN A NUTSHELL

CAPTURING THE ESSENCE OF LIFE
THROUGH QUOTES AND POETRY

AVINASH SINGH

Contents

Contents

Contents

1. Life

"Life is not just a journey, it's a adventure."
"Life is not just about the destination, it's about the journey."
"Life is not just about getting things done, it's about making memories."
"Life is not just about what you achieve, it's about who you become."
"Life is not just about what you accumulate, it's about what you give."
"Life is not just about reaching the top, it's about climbing the mountain."
"Life is not just about finding happiness, it's about creating it."
"Life is not a journey to be rushed, but a story to be written."

Life is a precious gift we receive, A journey that we are meant to weave, It's a canvas that we must paint, With colours bright and shades so quaint.

Life is a story that we must tell, A path that we must walk so well, It's a chance to make every moment count, And to leave behind a legacy that will amount.

Life is a melody that we must sing, A song that makes our spirits ring, It's a dance that we must learn to move, And to find our rhythm and our groove.

So let us live our life with grace, And embrace every challenge we face, For in the end, it's not the length that counts, But the depth and quality of the life that amounts.

2. Love

"Love is not just a feeling, it's a choice to care for another person every day."
"Love is an adventure, not a destination."
"The greatest happiness in life is the conviction that we are loved."
"Love is not what we have, but what we give."
"Love is not just a word, it's a verb. It's something we do, not just something we feel."
"The best love is the kind that awakens the soul and makes us reach for more, that plants a fire in our hearts and brings peace to our minds."
"Love is not just about finding someone who completes you, it's about finding someone who accepts and loves you for who you are."

Love is a flame that burns so bright, It fills our hearts with pure delight, It's a feeling that cannot be denied, A force that keeps us alive inside.

Love is the sun that warms the earth, The joy that gives our life its worth, It's a gift that we must cherish each day, And never let it fade away.

Love is the wind that lifts us high, The strength that helps us touch the sky, It's a bond that connects us all, And gives us the power to stand tall.

So let your heart be filled with love, And let it guide you from above, For with love, we can conquer all, And rise above every fall.

3. Intimacy

"Intimacy is not just about physical touch, it's about emotional and spiritual connection."
"Intimacy is the art of being together and being vulnerable, of sharing our hearts and souls with each other."
"Intimacy is not just about getting close, it's about staying close."
"Intimacy is the bond that holds two hearts together and makes life a beautiful journey."
"Intimacy is not just about physical pleasure, it's about experiencing true joy and happiness with another person."
"Intimacy is the foundation of a strong and lasting relationship, where two people can trust, support, and care for each other."
"Intimacy is not just about being intimate with one person, it's about being intimate with the world and all of life."

Intimacy is a sacred bond, A connection that we all respond, It's a closeness that we must cherish, And a bond that we must nourish.

Intimacy is the gift of trust, A place where we can be our truest, It's a refuge that we can rely on, and a bond that we can never con.

Intimacy is the warmth of touch, A feeling that we all love so much, It's a connection that we can't resist, And a bond that we can't dismiss.

So let us embrace intimacy with care, and let our hearts be open and bare, For in that bond, we find our worth, And in the end, we live a life of great mirth.

4. Spirituality

"Spirituality is not just about religion, it's about finding a connection with something greater than ourselves."
"Spirituality is the path to inner peace and happiness, to finding meaning and purpose in life."
"Spirituality is not just about knowing, it's about experiencing the divine within us and around us."
"Spirituality is the journey of the soul, a quest for understanding and enlightenment."
"Spirituality is not just about the destination, it's about the journey and the growth that comes from it."
"Spirituality is the connection between our mind, body, and spirit, and the realization of our place in the universe."
"Spirituality is not just about the journey, it's about the relationships we build and the love we share along the way."

Spirituality is the journey of the soul, A quest to help us reach our goal, It's a path that we all must find, And a journey that helps us to unwind.

Spirituality is the art of inner peace, A way to make our worries cease, It's a practice that we must cultivate, And a journey that we must not be late.

Spirituality is the search for meaning, A way to find out what's worth believing, It's a quest that we must undertake, And a journey that we must not forsake.

So let us seek spirituality with our heart, And let it be our guide from the start, For in that journey, we find our way, And in the end, we live a life with great sway.

5. Human Values

"Values are not just principles to live by, they are the foundation of who we are."
"Values are the guiding lights in our lives, showing us the way to make a positive impact in the world."
"Values are not just beliefs, they are the actions that we take every day to make a difference."
"Values are the seeds of greatness, that when nurtured, can bloom into a beautiful and fulfilling life."
"Values are not just what we hold dear, they are what make us human, and give us purpose and meaning."
"Values are the keys to unlocking our potential, to discovering our gifts and talents, and to making a positive impact in the world."
"Values are not just ideas, they are the living, breathing expression of our beliefs, and the driving force behind our actions."

Human values are the pillars of our soul, The guideposts that help us reach our goal, They are the light that leads us through the dark, And the compass that keeps us on the mark.

Human values are the virtues that we cherish, The morals that make our character flourish, They are the standards that we hold dear, And the principles that keep our path clear.

Human values are the essence of our being, The qualities that make us more than fleeting, They are the heart that beats within our chest, And the wisdom that helps us to do our best.

So let us uphold human values with pride, And let them be our strength and our guide, For in those values, we find our worth, And in the end, we live a life of great mirth.

6. Trust

"Trust is not just about believing in someone, it's about giving them the power to hurt you."

"Trust is the foundation of any strong relationship, and the key to unlocking its full potential."

"Trust is not just about the absence of fear, it's about the presence of hope."

"Trust is the currency of the soul, something that is earned and not easily given."

"Trust is not just about taking a leap of faith, it's about being willing to fall, and then being caught."

"Trust is the glue that holds us together, binding us to others and helping us to weather life's storms."

"Trust is not just about being open and vulnerable, it's about being willing to take a risk and reap the rewards."

*Trust is a bond that ties us tight, A truth that brings us into the light,
It's a faith that we must impart, And a bond that we must restart.*

*Trust is a choice that we make each day, A journey that leads us to a
brighter way, It's a step that we must take with care, And a bond that
we must never tear.*

*Trust is a bridge that spans the divide, A connection that helps us to
confide, It's a promise that we must uphold, And a treasure that is
more than gold.*

*So let us build trust with every breath, And let our words be filled
with depth, For in that trust, we find our worth, And in the end, we
live a life of mirth.*

7. Heartbreak

"Heartbreak is not just the end of a relationship, it's the end of a dream."
"Heartbreak is a teacher, showing us what we truly deserve and what we are willing to accept."
"Heartbreak is not just a feeling, it's a process, one that takes time, patience, and self-reflection."
"Heartbreak is a reminder of our own strength, and a testament to the resilience of the human spirit."
"Heartbreak is not just a loss, it's an opportunity to grow, to heal, and to find love again."
"Heartbreak is a chance to rediscover ourselves, to explore new paths, and to embrace new possibilities."
"Heartbreak is not just a heartache, it's a journey, one that takes us from pain to growth and from darkness to light."

Heartbreak is a wound that cuts so deep, A pain that never seems to sleep, It's a sorrow that we cannot contain, And a memory that leaves a stain.

Heartbreak is a void we cannot fill, A hurt that never seems to still, It's a burden that we cannot bear, And a wound that we cannot repair.

Heartbreak is a loss that we must mourn, A hurt that cannot be simply borne, It's a journey that we must tread, And a pain that never seems to shed.

So let us heal from heartbreak's pain, And let the hurt not be in vain, For in that pain, we find our strength, And in the end, we go to greater lengths

8. Overthinking

"Overthinking is not just a bad habit, it's a prison that keeps us from living in the moment."
"Overthinking is like being stuck in your own head, constantly second-guessing yourself and missing out on life."
"Overthinking is not just a waste of time, it's a source of anxiety and stress, clouding our judgment and inhibiting our action."
"Overthinking is a trap, one that keeps us stuck in the past or fearful of the future, instead of embracing the present."
"Overthinking is not just a problem, it's a choice, and one that we have the power to change."
"Overthinking is a barrier, blocking our path to happiness and fulfilment, and preventing us from realizing our full potential."
"Overthinking is not just a symptom, it's a disease, one that we can cure by embracing mindfulness and living in the present."

*Overthinking is a storm within, A tempest that makes our head spin,
It's a burden that we can't ignore, And a worry that we can't deplore.*

*Overthinking is a trap we weave, A web that never lets us leave, It's a
maze that we cannot escape, And a thought that we cannot reshape.*

*Overthinking is a thief of time, A prison that we cannot climb, It's a
weight that we cannot bear, And a thought that we cannot repair.*

*So let us break free from overthinking's grasp, And let our mind be at
peace at last, For in that peace, we find our way, And in the end, we
live a life with no dismay.*

9. Growth

"Growth is not just about getting bigger, it's about becoming better."
"Growth is the process of turning dreams into reality and turning potential into performance."
"Growth is not just a destination, it's a journey, one that requires commitment, discipline, and perseverance."
"Growth is a never-ending process, one that challenges us to continuously evolve and improve."
"Growth is not just a result, it's a mindset, one that celebrates progress and embraces change."
"Growth is a reward, one that brings us closer to our goals, and one that brings us closer to ourselves."
"Growth is not just a journey, it's a lifestyle, one that helps us to live life to the fullest and to achieve our full potential."

Growth is a process of becoming more, A journey that we must all explore, It's a transformation of our soul, And a journey that makes us whole.

Growth is a challenge that we must face, A way to step out of our own space, It's a path that we must embrace, And a journey that we cannot replace.

Growth is a journey that takes us far, A way to find out who we truly are, It's a process that never ends, And a journey that always amends.

So let us embrace growth with open arms, And let it bring us to new charms, For in that growth, we find our truth, And in the end, we live a life of proof.

10. Wisdom

"Wisdom is not just knowing what to do, it's knowing when to do it."

"Wisdom is not just a collection of knowledge, it's a way of life, one that is built on understanding, compassion, and empathy."

"Wisdom is not just about having answers, it's about asking the right questions."

"Wisdom is a journey, one that requires us to continuously seek truth and meaning, and to grow and evolve."

"Wisdom is not just a matter of intelligence, it's a matter of experience, and one that is acquired through living and learning."

"Wisdom is a treasure, one that is priceless, and one that we should constantly strive to acquire."

"Wisdom is not just a gift, it's a responsibility, one that we must pass on to future generations, and one that we must use to make the world a better place."

Wisdom is a light that shines so bright, A truth that brings us into the light, It's a voice that speaks with timeless grace, And a guide that helps us find our place.

Wisdom is a path that we must tread, A journey that leads to our own stead, It's a map that helps us navigate, And a compass that keeps us straight.

Wisdom is a gift that we receive, A knowledge that helps us to believe, It's a wisdom that we must impart, And a treasure that lies within our heart.

So let us seek wisdom with an open mind, And let it guide us through life's grind, For in that wisdom, we find our way, And in the end, we live a life with no dismay.

11. Art of Living

"The art of living is not just about existing, it's about experiencing life to the fullest."
"The art of living is not just about doing what makes you happy, it's about doing what is right."
"The art of living is not just about finding joy, it's about finding meaning and purpose."
"The art of living is not just about embracing the good times, it's about facing the challenges with courage and grace."
"The art of living is not just about enjoying the present, it's about creating a future that you can be proud of."
"The art of living is a journey, one that requires us to continuously grow, learn, and evolve."

The art of living is to find our path, A way to navigate life's twists and math, It's a quest for meaning and for grace, And a journey that we all must face.

The art of living is to live with joy, A way to embrace life's every ploy, It's a celebration of our human form, And a testament to the love that we adorn.

The art of living is to learn to grow, A way to evolve and let our soul glow, It's a process of becoming and of change, And a transformation that we must arrange.

The art of living is to love with care, A way to give and to always share, It's a commitment to the ones we hold, And a way to create memories bold.

So let us embrace the art of living with zest, And let our life be a canvas that we express, For in that art, we find our true self, And in the end, we leave a life well lived.

12. Friends

"Friends are not just people we know, they are people who understand us and accept us just the way we are."
"Friends are not just companions, they are the family we choose for ourselves."
"Friends are not just there for the good times, they are there for the tough times as well."
"Friends are not just sources of support, they are sources of inspiration and motivation."
"Friends are not just mirrors, they are windows, allowing us to see the world from a new perspective."
"Friends are not just the icing on the cake, they are the cake itself, giving life its flavour and meaning."
"Friends are not just blessings, they are treasures, and ones that we should hold dear to our hearts."

Friends are the stars that light up our night, A constellation that makes our world bright, They're the laughter that echoes in our soul, And the warmth that makes us feel whole.

Friends are the pillars that hold us strong, A bond that can never go wrong, They're the kindness that we always receive, And the support that helps us believe.

Friends are the memories that we cherish, A story that we will forever relish, They're the adventure that we embark, And the journey that leaves a mark.

So let us treasure our friends with care, And let their love always be there, For in our friends, we find our true gold, And in the end, their value cannot be told.

13. Family

"Family is not just about blood, it's about love, loyalty, and a bond that lasts a lifetime."

"Family is not just where we come from, it's where we belong."

"Family is not just a place of comfort, it's a place of strength."

"Family is not just a source of support, it's a source of inspiration and motivation."

"Family is not just a shelter from the storm, it's a safe haven for the soul."

"Family is not just a network of relationships, it's a tapestry of memories and traditions."

"Family is not just a group of people, it's a community of love and compassion."

Family is a bond that cannot be broken, A love that keeps us warm and unshaken, It's a home that we can always find, And a shelter that is always kind.

Family is a tree that roots us deep, A strength that we can always keep, It's a legacy that we inherit, And a legacy that we must merit.

Family is a circle that surrounds, A support that forever abounds, It's a place that we belong and thrive, And a comfort that helps us to survive.

So let us cherish our family with care, And embrace the love that they always share, For in that family, we find our heart, And in the end, we are never apart

14. Respect

"Respect is not just a word, it's a way of life."
"Respect is not just about being polite, it's about valuing the worth of others."
"Respect is not just about listening, it's about understanding."
"Respect is not just about being kind, it's about being humble."
"Respect is not just about being tolerant, it's about embracing diversity."
"Respect is not just about being honest, it's about being truthful and fair."
"Respect is not just about being courteous, it's about treating others the way you want to be treated."

Respect is a bridge that we must build, A way to connect and to fulfill, It's a bond that we must create, And a virtue that we must cultivate.

Respect is a gift that we must give, A value that helps us to live, It's a dignity that we must uphold, And a courtesy that we must unfold.

Respect is a choice that we must make, A decision that we cannot fake, It's a reflection of our character, And a measure of our honor.

So let us show respect to all we meet, And let it guide us through life's heat, For in that respect, we find our grace, And in the end, we leave a noble trace

15. Money

"Money is not just a means of exchange, it's a measure of value."

"Money is not just a source of security, it's a source of freedom."

"Money is not just a symbol of wealth, it's a symbol of opportunity."

"Money is not just a tool, it's a measure of success."

"Money is not just a way to buy things, it's a way to create value."

"Money is not just a way to keep score, it's a way to pursue happiness."

"Money is not just a means to an end, it's a means to a better life."

Money is a means to an end, A tool that we can always spend, It's a bridge that takes us from here to there, And helps us reach for the things we care.

Money is a symbol of value and wealth, A measure of our financial health, It's a currency that we exchange, For goods and services that we arrange.

Money is a force that drives our goals, A power that can make us whole, It's a reward for our hard work and time, And a way to make our dreams climb.

But let us not be consumed by greed, And let money not be our only need, For in the end, it's the love and the care, That truly enrich our life's fare.

16. Adventure

"Adventure is not just a journey, it's a state of mind."
"Adventure is not just about taking risks, it's about embracing uncertainty."
"Adventure is not just about exploring new places, it's about discovering new perspectives."
"Adventure is not just about the destination, it's about the journey."
"Adventure is not just about pushing boundaries, it's about expanding horizons."
"Adventure is not just about the thrill of the moment, it's about the memories that last a lifetime."
"Adventure is not just about seeking excitement, it's about seeking self-discovery."

Adventure is a call to the wild, A journey that leaves us beguiled, It's a quest for the unknown and new, A chance to learn and to renew.

Adventure is a path to be brave, A way to push beyond the safe, It's a risk that we must take and believe, And to embrace what we can achieve.

Adventure is a test of our will, A challenge that can make us thrill, It's a story that we must create, And a memory that will never abate.

So let us venture beyond our fears, And explore the world with our ears, For in adventure, we find our true soul, And in the end, we become whole.

17. Inner Peace

"Inner peace is not just a feeling, it's a state of mind."
"Inner peace is not just about being calm, it's about being content."
"Inner peace is not just about letting go, it's about finding balance."
"Inner peace is not just about finding stillness, it's about finding clarity."
"Inner peace is not just about avoiding conflict, it's about resolving it."
"Inner peace is not just about being free from stress, it's about being free from worry."
"Inner peace is not just about being quiet, it's about being at ease with who you are."

*Inner peace is a gentle breeze, A stillness that brings us to our knees,
It's a calm that settles deep within, And frees us from the world's
constant din.*

*Inner peace is a light that shines so bright, A tranquility that
illuminates the night, It's a space that we can always find, And a
harbor for our restless mind.*

*Inner peace is a grace that we receive, A gift that helps us to believe,
It's a source of strength and of power, And a refuge in life's stormy hour.*

*So let us seek the peace that lies within, And let it guide us through
thick and thin, For in that peace, we find our true self, And in the
end, we are at peace with ourselves.*

18. Affection

"Affection is the glue that binds relationships together."
"Affection is the sweetest thing that can happen to a human being."
"Affection is the magic ingredient that turns strangers into friends and friends into family."
"Affection is the language of the heart, spoken without words."
"Affection is a priceless gift that costs nothing to give, but is worth everything to receive."
"Affection is the sun that warms the soul and the rain that nourishes it."
"Affection is the music of life, it soothes the soul and makes the heart sing."
"Affection is the spark that ignites the fire of love and the ember that keeps it burning."

Affection is a gentle breeze, A soothing touch that puts us at ease, It's the warmth of a loving embrace, That brings a smile to our face.

Affection is the light in our eyes, The bond that connects us to the skies, It's the sweet melody of a song, That lifts our spirits all day long.

Affection is the beauty of a flower, The magic that gives us the power, To believe in the goodness of life, And banish all worry and strife.

So cherish the affection in your heart, And let it be your guiding star, For it will lead you to happiness and peace, And make all your troubles cease.

19. Success

"Success is not final, failure is not fatal: it is the courage to continue that counts."
"Success is not the key to happiness. Happiness is the key to success. If you love what you are doing, you will be successful."
"Success is liking yourself, liking what you do, and liking how you do it."
"Success is not measured by what you accomplish, but by the opposition you have encountered, and the courage with which you have maintained the struggle against overwhelming odds."
"Success is not in what you have, but who you are."
"Success is a journey, not a destination. The doing is often more important than the outcome."
"The road to success is always under construction."
"Success is when preparation meets opportunity."
"Success is not about being the best. It's about always getting better."
"Success is the sum of small efforts, repeated day in and day out."

Success is a journey, not a destination, A path that's filled with determination, It's a journey that we must all embark, And a journey that must leave a mark.

Success is a victory that we win, A battle that we must fight from within, It's a triumph that we must achieve, And a victory that we must perceive.

Success is a state of mind and being, A feeling that fills our hearts with meaning, It's a joy that we must never lose, And a gift that we must always choose.

So let us strive for success with all our might, And let us keep our goals in sight, For in that journey, we find our worth, And in the end, we live a life of great mirth.

20. Failure

Failure is a detour, not a dead-end street."
"Success is not final, failure is not fatal: it is the courage to continue that counts."
"Failure is simply the opportunity to begin again, this time more intelligently."
"Failure is a part of success. There is no such thing as a bed of roses all your life. But failure will never stand in the way of success if you learn from it."
"The only real failure is the failure to try."
"Don't fear failure. Fear being in the exact same place next year as you are today."
"Failure is not falling down but refusing to get up."
"Success is going from failure to failure without losing your enthusiasm."
"Failure is not the opposite of success, it's a part of success."
"The only way to avoid failure is to never try anything new."

Failure is not the end, but just a start, A chance to learn, to grow, to play a part, For every fall is just a stepping stone, To help us rise and stand tall, alone.

In every failure, there's a lesson to be learned, A chance to grow, and new skills to be earned, For it's in those moments of defeat and despair, That we learn to rise above, and show we care.

So let us embrace failure with open arms, And let it teach us its many charms, For in that journey, we find our worth, And in the end, we live a life of great mirth

21. Pain

"The pain you feel today is the strength you feel tomorrow."
"Pain is inevitable. Suffering is optional."
"The pain of the mind is worse than the pain of the body."
"The greater your capacity to love, the greater your capacity to feel the pain."
"Pain is temporary, but the pride of overcoming it lasts forever."
"Pain is not a punishment, pleasure is not a reward."
"Pain makes you stronger, fear makes you braver, heartbreak makes you wiser."
"Pain is a reminder that you are still alive."
"Pain is a gift. Without it, we'd forget how much we need each other."
"Pain is a part of life, but suffering is optional."

Pain, oh pain, you visitor unwelcome, You come to us uninvited, and leave us broken, You twist and turn, and gnaw at our hearts, And tear our world apart, in tiny little parts.

Yet through your agony, we learn to see, The beauty of the world, and what it means to be, For pain is but a teacher, that shows us the way, To live our lives with courage, and love every day.

So though you hurt us, and make us cry, We know that through your lessons, we will learn to fly, To reach for the stars, and chase our dreams, And live a life full of joy, and endless gleams.

So pain, oh pain, we welcome you still, For through your lessons, we learn to heal, To become better, stronger, and wiser too, And live a life that's full of love, and beauty anew.

22. Meditation

"Meditation is the journey to your inner self."
"The best way to begin meditation is to stop thinking about it."
"Meditation is not a way of making your mind quiet. It's a way of entering into the quiet that's already there."
"Meditation is not a task, it's a state of being."
"In meditation, we find the silence that makes us whole."
"Meditation is the art of paying attention to the present moment."
"Meditation is the key to unlock the doors of your mind."
"Meditation is the ultimate adventure, a journey to the center of your own being."
"Meditation is the medicine that can heal the wounds of the soul."
"Meditation is not an escape from reality, it's a way of embracing it."

In stillness I sit, in silence I breathe, As I close my eyes, my soul finds its reprieve, My mind begins to slow, my heart begins to open, And in the quiet of my being, a peace unspoken.

The world fades away, as I focus on my breath, The rise and fall of my chest, a dance of life and death, My thoughts begin to clear, my worries start to fade, And in the stillness of my soul, a light is made.

For in the depths of meditation, a truth is found, A connection to the universe, that knows no bounds, A oneness with all things, a love that's pure and true, A clarity of purpose, that shines like morning dew.

So I sit in meditation, and I let my spirit soar, I open up my heart, and I let it explore, The infinite universe that dwells within, And I find my truest self, as I breathe in and out again

23. Goodbye

"Goodbyes are not forever, they are not the end; it simply means I'll miss you until we meet again."

"Saying goodbye doesn't mean anything. It's the time we spent together that matters, not how we left it."

"Goodbye is not a word, it's a sentence. It's a beginning and an end."

"The hardest part of saying goodbye is the fear of never seeing them again."

"It's not the goodbye that hurts, but the flashbacks that follow."

"Goodbye is like a stormy cloud, it comes without warning and leaves you drenched in tears."

"Goodbyes make you think. They make you realize what you've had, what you've lost, and what you've taken for granted."

"Goodbyes are not easy, but sometimes they are necessary. They remind us of what's important, and give us the strength to move on."

"When we say goodbye, it's not the end of a journey, but the beginning of a new one."

"The pain of saying goodbye is a reminder that we are capable of love, and that is something to be cherished."

Goodbye, my friend, it's time to part, Though it hurts, it's a brand new start. We laughed, we cried, we shared our lives, And now it's time to say goodbye.

The memories we've made will never fade, And the love we shared will always stay. We'll treasure the moments that we had, And hold them close when we feel sad.

The time has come to say farewell, Though we'll keep in touch, I can always tell. Our paths may lead us far apart, But the love we shared will keep us close at heart.

So here's to you, my dear friend, May your journey be filled with joy until the end. And though we're saying goodbye today, Our friendship will never fade away.

24. Honesty

"Honesty is the first chapter in the book of wisdom."
"Honesty is the best policy, not just because it's morally right, but because it's the most effective strategy for success."
"Honesty is not just about telling the truth, it's also about being true to yourself."
"Honesty is a very expensive gift. Don't expect it from cheap people."
"Honesty is a rare and precious commodity. Those who possess it are worth their weight in gold."
"Honesty is the foundation of all human relationships. Without it, there can be no trust, no love, and no respect."
"Honesty is the key to unlocking the door to true happiness and inner peace."
"Honesty may not always be the easiest path, but it is always the right one."
"Honesty is a reflection of your character. It is the mark of a truly good person."
"Honesty is not just a virtue, it's a way of life."

Honesty is the purest of deeds, A virtue that everyone needs. It's the cornerstone of trust and respect, And the foundation of all that is correct.

Honesty is the truth that we speak, The promises we make that we'll keep. It's the way we act and the things we do, Reflecting the values that we hold true.

Honesty is the light that guides, When darkness falls and doubt resides. It's the compass that always points north, And the quality that sets us forth.

Honesty is a rare and precious gem, To be cherished, valued, and treasured like them. It's a mark of integrity and a sign of worth, And the quality that defines our birth.

So let us always be honest and true, And live our lives with integrity through and through. For honesty is the path to true success, And the key to a life that's truly blessed.

25. Hope

"Hope is the light that shines in the darkest of moments."
"Hope is the thing with feathers that perches in the soul and sings the tune without the words and never stops at all."
"Hope is the anchor that keeps us from drifting in the storms of life."
"Hope is the power that enables us to overcome the obstacles we face."
"Hope is the whisper that says, 'you can do it', when all seems lost."
"Hope is the belief that the future holds something better for us."
"Hope is the fire that burns within us, giving us the strength to carry on."
"Hope is the beacon that guides us to safety, even in the midst of the storm."
"Hope is the hand that reaches out to pull us up when we fall."
"Hope is the reminder that no matter how bad things seem, there is always a chance for something good to happen."

When darkness falls and shadows loom, And all around is deepening gloom, When troubles come and fears take hold, And the path ahead seems rough and cold.

That's when hope must take the lead, A light to follow, a friend indeed. It's the promise of a brighter day, A ray of sunshine along the way.

Hope is the spark that ignites the flame, That sets our souls and spirits aflame. It's the whisper of a better tomorrow, A chance for joy, free from sorrow.

With hope as our guide, we can face any trial, Knowing that in the end, we'll emerge with a smile. For hope is the beacon that leads us through the night, And the force that makes everything right.

So hold on to hope, with all your might, And let it guide you through the darkest night. For with hope as your ally, you'll never lose your way, And the future will be brighter, come what may.

26. Dream

"A dream is a wish your heart makes."
"Dreams are the roadmap to the future."
"All our dreams can come true, if we have the courage to pursue them."
"Dreams are the seeds of greatness."
"Dream big and chase your dreams until they come true."
"Your dreams are the key to unlocking your full potential."
"Dreams are the wings that take us to new heights."
"Never stop dreaming, for dreams are the fuel that powers the soul."
"Dreams are the canvas on which we paint our future."
"The biggest adventure you can ever take is to live the life of your dreams."

Dreams are the whispers of the heart, The longing of the soul to depart, From the mundane and the routine, To a world of magic and unseen.

Dreams are the colors of the mind, The canvas on which we find, The path to a brighter day, Where troubles and worries fade away.

Dreams are the fuel that ignites, The passion that fuels our flights, To the sky and beyond, we go, With dreams as our wings and the wind as our foe.

Dreams are the seed that we sow, The hope that keeps us on the go, For in dreams, we see the light, That leads us to the end of the night.

So dream on, dreamer, and never stop, For dreams are the key to unlock, The door to a life of wonder and joy, And the road to a future bright and giude

27. Kindness

"Kindness is the sunshine in which virtue grows."
"Be kind, for everyone you meet is fighting a battle you know nothing about."
"A single act of kindness throws out roots in all directions, and the roots spring up and make new trees."
"Kindness is a language that the deaf can hear and the blind can see."
"The best way to find yourself is to lose yourself in the service of others."
"No act of kindness, no matter how small, is ever wasted."
"Spread love and kindness wherever you go, for it is the way to a brighter world."
"Kindness is the key to unlocking the doors of the heart."
"In a world where you can be anything, be kind."
"The true test of a person's character is how they treat those who can do nothing for them."

Kindness is a balm that heals the soul, A light that brightens up the darkest hole, A gift that costs us nothing to give, And yet, it is the most precious way to live.

Kindness is the gentle touch of a hand, The warm embrace of a friend who understands, The words of comfort in a time of need, The act of grace that makes hearts bleed.

Kindness is the melody of the heart, The symphony of love that never departs, The harmony that brings us all together, And makes this world a place of joy forever.

So let us all be kind in every way, And make the world a brighter place today, For kindness is the key to unlock, The doors of hope and love, and heal the world's every block.

28. Power

"Power is not control, it is the ability to empower others."
"True power comes not from wealth or might, but from love and light."
"Power is the ability to make things happen, but true power is the ability to make good things happen."
"The true measure of power is not in how much we can acquire, but in how much we can give."
"The greatest power is not in force, but in understanding."
"The power to change the world lies in every single one of us."
"True power is not in imposing our will on others, but in empowering them to achieve their full potential."
"Power is not in the title, it is in the ability to inspire others."
"Power is not a license to do whatever we want, but a responsibility to do what is right."
"The greatest power is in the ability to love, forgive and show compassion to others."

Power is not in what you hold, But in what you give away, Not in the force of your control, But in the words you choose to say.

Power is not in titles or rank, But in the kindness of your heart, Not in the treasures in your bank, But in how you set others apart.

Power is not in how much you take, But in how much you can let go, Not in the threats that you make, But in the peace that you can show.

So let your power be in your love, And in your willingness to serve, For in the end, it's what we give, That truly leaves a lasting curve.

29. Missing

"Missing someone isn't about how long it's been since you've seen them, or the amount of time since you've talked. It's about that very moment when you're doing something, and you wish they were right there with you."
"Missing someone is your heart's way of reminding you that you love them."
"Missing someone is a part of loving them."
"Missing someone gets easier every day because even though you are one day further from the last time you saw them, you are one day closer to the next time you will."
"Missing someone is not a weakness, it's a sign that you have someone special in your life whom you cherish and love."

I miss your smile, your laugh, your touch, The way you'd always cheer me up. I miss the sound of your sweet voice, And how you'd make my heart rejoice.

I miss the way you'd look at me, And how you'd always let me be. I miss the warmth of your embrace, And the feeling of your gentle face.

I miss the way we used to be, The way we'd talk, the way we'd dream. I miss the moments that we shared, And how you showed me that you cared.

But though you're gone, I won't forget, The love we had, the memories set. And though I miss you every day, In my heart, you'll always stay

30. Truth

"The truth may hurt for a little while, but a lie hurts forever."
"You can ignore the truth, but it won't go away."
"The truth will always be the truth, even if no one believes it."
"The truth is like a lion; you don't have to defend it. Let it loose, it will defend itself."
"The truth is rarely pure and never simple."

Truth stands like a mountain tall, Unwavering and unchanging through it all. It's the one thing that cannot be moved, No matter how much it's tried to be proved.

It may be hard to face at times, But truth never falls for anyone's lies. It stands alone, stark and bare, A light that cuts through darkness and despair.

It's not always what we want to hear, But truth is what we must hold dear. For when we speak it, we are free, And the truth shall always set us free.

31. Dedication

"Dedication is the fuel that powers the engine of success."
"Dedication means putting in the time and effort to do something right, no matter how long it takes."
"Dedication is the difference between a dream and a reality."
"Success is the result of hard work, dedication, and persistence."
"Dedication is not what others expect of you, it is what you expect of yourself."

Dedication is a flame that burns within, A drive that pushes us to always win. It's the fuel that keeps us going strong, Through the battles, the struggles, and the long.

It's the steady hand that guides our way, The compass that leads us every day. It's the voice that whispers, "don't give in," And the heart that keeps on beating within.

Dedication is the heart of our success, The key to achieving what we profess. It's the passion that ignites our fire, And the unwavering will that takes us higher.

So let us cherish dedication deep, And let it guide us as we leap. For with it, we can achieve our dreams, And soar higher than ever it seems.

32. Courage

"Courage is not the absence of fear, but the triumph over it."

"Courage is the strength to stand up when it's easier to give up."

"Courage is not the roar of a lion, but the calm determination of a lamb."

"Courage is the willingness to take action despite the fear of failure."

"Courage is the power to let go of the familiar and embrace the new."

"You gain strength, courage, and confidence by every experience in which you really stop to look fear in the face."

"Courage is not something you have, it's something you earn."

"Be strong and courageous, for you never know who you are inspiring."

Courage is not the absence of fear, But the strength to push through and persevere. It's the fire that burns in the heart, Giving us the will to make a fresh start.

It's the voice that tells us to take a stand, To hold our ground and make a demand. It's the warrior's spirit that never fades, Even when the path ahead is fraught with shades.

It's the spark that ignites our inner flame, And the force that helps us rise above the pain. It's the belief that we can face any challenge, And the power to transform our fate and arrange.

So let us cherish courage in our soul, And let it guide us as we move toward our goal. For with it, we can conquer every foe, And create a future that we can proudly show.

33. Attitude

"Attitude is a little thing that makes a big difference."
"Your attitude determines your altitude."
"Your attitude, not your aptitude, will determine your altitude."
"Attitude is a choice. Happiness is a choice. Optimism is a choice. Kindness is a choice. Giving is a choice. Respect is a choice. Whatever choice you make makes you. Choose wisely."
"Your attitude is like a box of crayons that color your world. Constantly color your picture gray, and your picture will always be bleak. Try adding some bright colors to the picture by including humor, and your picture begins to lighten up."
"The only disability in life is a bad attitude."
"Your attitude is the paintbrush of your mind. It can color any situation."
"A positive attitude can really make dreams come true - it did for me."

Attitude is the way we choose, To face life's joys and blues. It's the lens through which we see, The world and all its mystery.

With a positive attitude we'll find, That life is good and fate is kind. But if we choose to be negative, We'll find the world to be quite oppressive.

So let's embrace an attitude of grace, And wear a smile upon our face. For life is what we make it to be, And a good attitude will set us free.

Thank You

Dear Readers, I wanted to take a moment to express my heartfelt gratitude to all of you .

I would also like to extend my thanks to those who have provided me with quotes and references that I have used in my writing. Your wisdom and insights have helped me to shape my ideas and communicate them more effectively.

I am truly grateful for the opportunity to share my thoughts and ideas with you, and I hope that my work has been able to provide value and meaning to your lives in some way. Thank you for your support and for being a part of this journey with me. With sincere thanks and appreciation,

Avinash Singh

* 9 7 9 8 8 8 8 9 7 5 8 0 9 9 *